DATE		

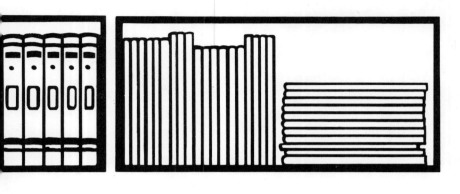

PUBLISHING CAREERS

MAGAZINES AND BOOKS

PHOTOGRAPHS
BY CHUCK
FREEDMAN

LONDON | 1978
NEW YORK
FRANKLIN WATTS

A Career Concise Guide

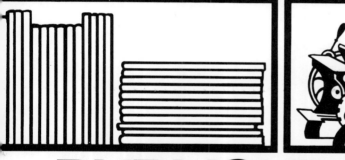

PUBLISHING
CAREERS
MAGAZINES AND BOOKS
by Charles Paul May

To Patty, Denny, Vaughn, and Aaron.
Also to Fred Graves and Frank Berge.

ACKNOWLEDGMENTS:

The author wishes to express his thanks to the
many people who helped gather information, in-
cluding Margaret Adams, Margaret Cosgrove,
Norma Dickey, Dina Donohue, Luke Feck, Martin
W. Goodman, Harold Grove, C. J. Hadley, Alex
Hood, Ed Kern, Grace Morgan, Marjorie Naughton,
Herman Stein, and Hal Wingo.

For their assistance in producing the photographs
for this book, the photographer thanks: Jane Gil-
christ of Sports Illustrated; Barthold Fles Literary
Agency; Louis Solovinsky of Time-Life.

Library of Congress Cataloging in Publication Data

May, Charles Paul.
    Publishing careers.

    (A Career concise guide)
    Bibliography: p.
    Includes index.
    SUMMARY: Describes the opportunities in and
the education and training required for a variety
of careers in publishing.
    1. Publishers and publishing—Vocational guid-
ance—Juvenile literature. [1. Publishers and publishing—Vocational guidance. 2. Vocational guid-
ance] I. Freedman, Chuck. II. Title.
Z278.M36   070.5'023   77–17955
ISBN 0–531–01422–3

Contents

Introduction

Publishing is defined in the dictionary as making something public—or generally known. This book is published to let you know what jobs in publishing are like, how much they pay, and how you can prepare yourself for one of them.

This book will describe jobs on magazines and in book publishing. You will find a section on each of them. There is also a short section on literary agencies. Simply for reasons of space, news magazines and newspapers are not included. They are a special part of publishing, generally called "journalism," and will soon have a career guide of their own.

The publishing field, like any other, changes from time to time. New jobs open up and others cease to exist. For example, type was originally made and set by hand. There were many jobs for people who did this work. Now automatic equipment does almost all of it. But other people, with special training, are needed to operate the equipment.

There may be more changes by the time you are ready for a job—certainly salaries will have changed. This book gives a general picture of the publishing field today, and of the career opportunities it offers.

EARLY PLANNING

If you think you are interested in a career in publishing, it's not too early to start planning for it. If you can visit a magazine or a book publisher, that will be a good start. If there are none in your neighborhood, your state university may have a university press, which would be worth seeing. You may be able to talk to someone there who will be well qualified to advise you, if you call or write for an appointment in advance.

Working on your school or college publications will give you good experience if you can fit it into your schedule. And don't limit yourself to editorial work. If you sell space for ads or schedule pictures for your senior yearbook, that's good experience too. In both book and magazine publishing it's important to understand all the work that goes into a publication.

Part-time or summer work with a local publisher is even better experience—if you are lucky enough to land a job. Education is especially important for those who are planning on a publishing career. Since words will be the tools of your trade, you will want to take all the English and writing courses offered at your school. Try to get a good dictionary of your own. And take typing if you can. Most people in publishing use a typewriter. It's another tool of the trade (and one which will also make your progress through school and college easier).

Plenty of free time for reading and exploring other interests is important too. Publishers need workers who are both well-educated and well-rounded people. So make a habit of spending some time browsing in libraries and bookstores. And take a critical look at the books you read. What do you think of this book? Do you like the type used? Is the jacket design attractive? Is it easy to understand? Is the index helpful? Just by being a critical reader you will begin to understand what makes a good book or magazine.

In publishing, any department may go by more than one name. This is also true of jobs. In an editorial department, new employees may be called editorial trainees, assistants to the editor, or simply assistants. Each magazine or book publisher will have its own name for a particular job, so you need to know something about what actual work is involved. While it gives typical job-titles, this book concentrates on what people *do* in magazine and book publishing.

MAGAZINE
PUBLISHING

About Magazines

When you stop at a corner newsstand, you find dozens of different magazines on display. Some may be more attractive to you than others. But each magazine was designed to catch the eye and to appeal to a particular group of people. Let's look at some of the many different types.

GENERAL MAGAZINES
All of the magazines found at the newsstand appeal to large (but special) groups of the general population, so they are called general magazines. *Good Housekeeping* is designed to appeal primarily to homemakers, *Ebony* to blacks, *Yachting* to sailors, *Sports Illustrated* to sports fans, *Mad* to madcaps, *Ms.* to women, and so on.

SPECIALIZED MAGAZINES
There are many other magazines that don't appear on the newsstand at all. They are usually sent directly to the reader. There are thousands of different specialized magazines.

Those of interest to people in one profession—medicine, teaching, archaeology, banking—are called **professional journals.** The ones that serve all the companies in a single industry, such as construction work or laundromats, are called **industrials,** or trade journals. Magazines put out by corporations for customers and dealers are known as **externals** because they go to interested people outside of (external to) the business firm itself. Some firms also produce magazines for the people working within the company. These are called **house organs.** Universities and other groups try to keep good writing alive by publishing magazines devoted to poetry, short stories, or essays. These literary journals are often called **the little magazines.** Religious publishing houses bring out magazines of interest to church members. Alumni or alumnae magazines are for the graduates of a particular college. There are innumerable magazines of this sort for special groups of readers.

JOBS ON MAGAZINES

Each of the magazines mentioned has been conceived, then produced, and then circulated. Most of them pay their way and earn their profits by selling space to advertisers. There are many different kinds of work involved in getting each magazine out. And the jobs on one magazine are not identical to the jobs on another magazine.

One helpful thing to know is what the major job areas in magazines are. No doubt you already know that magazines have to be edited. The *editorial department* includes all those who provide editorial material (as opposed to the advertisements). It includes the *art department,* sometimes called *design* or *layout,* and is responsible for the magazine's appearance. But the editorial department is just one part of the magazine. The *production department* is responsible for producing the magazine. The *advertising department* persuades businesses and corporations to buy space in the magazine for their ads. The *promotion department* publicizes the magazine. And while all these departments go about their work, the *circulation* (or *distribution*) *department* arranges for the magazine to reach the people who will read it.

**A negative reader
checks a slide,
using a lightboard.**

PUBLISHER

In magazine publishing, the head of the firm is called the publisher. The person in this position has often worked his or her way up through the advertising department. Perhaps the publisher has been a successful advertising manager. The magazine publisher's primary concern is profits. These profits come principally from advertising revenues. The publisher is responsible to the stockholders or owners of the firm for a healthy balance sheet.

Few people spend their lives working for the same firm— or even in the same field. If you think you are interested in a particular area of publishing—art, for example—be sure to read the section on book design departments as well as the one describing art department jobs on magazines. You will have a better idea of job opportunities if you read both sections.

Editorial Department

On most magazines there is a managing editor who coordinates all these sections and reports to the top editor of the magazine. A small magazine may have one editor, an assistant or two, and perhaps some secretarial help. On a larger magazine the editorial department (sometimes called "edit" for short) may have several sections. A woman's magazine may have a fashion section, a decorating section, a food section, and a fiction section, with an editor in charge of each one and a managing editor in overall charge.

THE EDITOR
The top editor, sometimes called "editor-in-chief," plans each issue of the magazine and manages, or oversees, the work of the department. The editor has the final say on what goes into the magazine. This person gives the go-ahead signal for story and picture assignments and approves or improves the final editing and **layouts.** On magazines, "story" means nonfiction articles as well as fiction; "pictures" includes all illustrative material—drawings, photographs, and so on; a "layout" is a rough sketch of a page showing the position of pictures and text.

OTHER EDITORS
Assisting the editor on a large magazine are subeditors with various titles (such as managing editor, executive editor,

etc.) They are referred to generally as "editors." One part of each editor's job is to plan stories and assign them to outside writers (with the approval of the managing editor). After the story or article has been written, the editor makes necessary changes and then returns the completed piece for the writer's approval. The more the final manuscript reads like the original in style and content, the more likely the author is to approve the changes. Good editors can generally improve a story while keeping the best qualities provided by the writer.

Almost no written material goes to the printer exactly as the author wrote it. This is particularly true of nonfiction—articles and essays. Editors try to make every story completely clear, interesting, accurate, and easy to read. Grammar is corrected if necessary, and sentence structure is improved. Factual mistakes are corrected, additional information may be added, and the spelling is checked.

CONTRIBUTING EDITORS

Some magazines employ outside editors who act as scouts: they think of good subjects for articles and find authors to write them. Occasionally contributing editors write articles themselves. These specialists may live almost anywhere, since they don't have to go to the magazine office every day. But it is usually necessary to have previous experience on the **staff** of a particular magazine in order to get a job like this.

EDITORIAL ASSISTANTS

Large magazines have editorial assistants who do research and check facts. Their job is to prove the accuracy of every statement in a story and to dig up more material on a subject

A researcher at Time-Life checking the facts and figures in an article. Each line of a piece in a Time-Life publication must be checked twice.

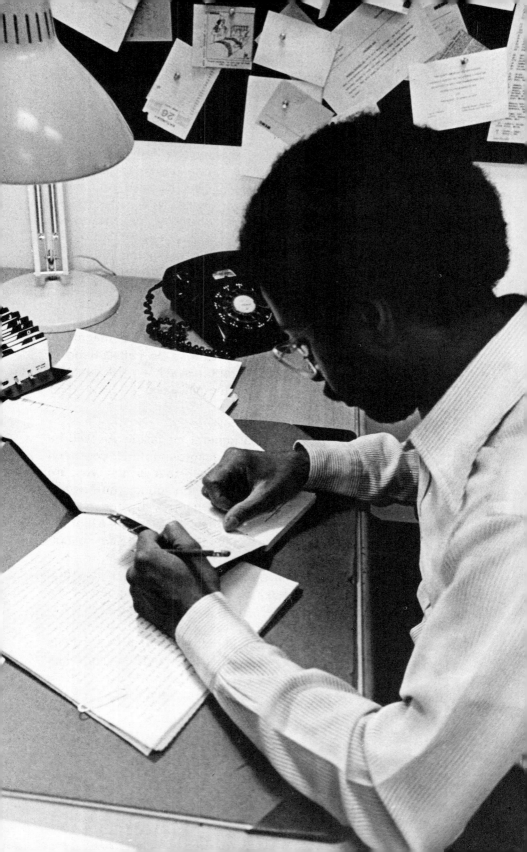

if it is needed. They make simple corrections themselves, and they give copy that needs rewriting to one of the editors.

COPY READERS

In publishing, the material to be printed is called **copy.** The time when that material must go to the printer is called the **closing** time. Weekly magazines, which have enormous amounts of copy to close in a very short time, have special **copy readers** who read everything going into the issue and check for grammar, spelling, etc. On smaller monthly magazines the editor and his or her assistants handle this job.

Another editorial job is proofreading. The printer sets copy into type. This printed material is sent back to the magazine along with the original copy. The printed sheets are known as **proofs.** The proofreader checks them against the original copy to be sure that they match. On a small magazine, anyone from a secretary to an editor may be called upon to read copy and check proofs. It requires a keen eye, and an ability to concentrate, to catch all the mistakes.

PREPARATION

In the editorial department of a general magazine you will be expected to have a good general background. First, you need expert command of the language, since that is how you are going to communicate with your readers; second, you need to be acquainted with all the subjects of interest to your readers, from science to art to politics. If you are also an expert in particular areas—rock music, ancient Greece, stamp collecting, sailing—that's all to the good.

How do you go about preparing yourself for a field that makes such broad demands? In order to be an expert in the use of words you will need all the courses you can take in English, literature, and writing. You will need to read widely. You will gain knowledge of a variety of subjects primarily by being curious about everything you see and do—and then following up on that curiosity. If you're a shell collector, find out where the nearest great collection is and go to see it. If you're a fan of rock music, talk to the experts you meet about the history of rock. None of your present enthusiasms is a waste of time if it adds to your store of knowledge.

Most editors are college graduates. Colleges and universities offer liberal arts programs, and some offer programs in journalism. A recent trend is to combine language arts, writing, journalism, and broadcasting in a program called communications. People hiring for magazines often prefer graduates with a liberal arts or communications background. They feel that journalism students may be too specifically trained for newspaper work.

GETTING STARTED

In any department of a magazine your first job will probably be one in which you learn while you work. In the editorial department you might start as a clerk or a secretary or an editorial assistant. You may be called a trainee or a copyboy or a copygirl. No matter what your title, you will now have a chance to learn about the editorial process. If you are a secretary, you will have a chance to see everything from writer's contracts to edited copy to captions for pictures. You will soon begin to see why a piece of text was changed in a particular way, how a caption was written in order to give the largest amount of information in the smallest amount of space. As an assistant you may be assigned to the letters-to-the-editor section, and have a hand in choosing the letters to run in the next issue. In the process you will learn about the many problems facing the editors in deciding what to use in a particular issue of a magazine. In any one of these jobs you will be learning. And you will be on the spot when a chance comes to move up.

REWARDS

Salaries in magazine publishing are higher in the major centers, such as New York, Boston, Toronto, Philadelphia, Chicago, and San Francisco—and salaries are higher for work on specialized magazines that require advanced degrees. New employees usually start at about $100 to $150 a week. After a year or two of experience, an editorial employee may look around for openings paying $200 a week or more, and seasoned editorial people earn more than $300. Contributing editors sometimes fare as well as editors in offices, depending on how much material they provide. Top editors receive $400 to $600 a week or more.

Art Department

Each magazine on display at the newsstand has a distinctive appearance—a style of its own. If you're a regular reader of *Rolling Stone* or *People,* you probably recognize a new issue instantly. The art department is responsible for this style and for maintaining it throughout each issue. The art department works closely with the editorial department and, in the case of general magazines, with circulation. Choosing a particular cover also has a direct bearing on circulation; some covers are more successful and sell more copies of the magazine at newsstands than others do.

ART DIRECTORS

The art director is the person responsible for the magazine's overall design and appearance. He or she works with the editors in planning each issue and deciding how articles and stories should be illustrated. The art director is also in charge of hiring the people in the art department, directing their work and choosing pictures and layouts to submit to the editor. The art director also looks at the work of **free-lance** artists and photographers and decides whether or not to suggest giving them assignments. Another responsibility is estimating expenses. If special effects result in extra costs, the art director and the editors decide whether they are worth the cost.

OCT 10

HEAD MOVE CUT
KILL LINE

① HAVE A WHALE 12
② OF A TIME 8
③ This is nine on ten Helvetica Demi Bold being set on the Videocomp. Photo
the Toronto war, while New York Islanders (ranked 1 ▶ FATTEN HELV BOLD
-18- ④ 1X 50

W
⑤

46
52
LINE

46

38

46

38

1
54

LAYOUT ARTISTS
A layout artist makes a detailed plan for each page of a magazine. This plan is called a layout. A sample, or **dummy** page, is marked to show the exact positions of text, ads, and pictures. The kind of type to be used is indicated. Illustrations are marked, or scaled, for size.

SPECIALISTS
Artwork sometimes requires the attention of people with special talents. Most magazines rely on free-lance specialists or commercial art studios, but a few have specialists on the staff.

If a photograph shows spots or scratches, a retoucher can paint them out. If there is an object that the editor doesn't want shown (such as a liquor bottle), a good retoucher can cause it to disappear by giving it a coating that will blend with the background. Retouchers are sometimes asked to make the people in nude pictures less naked by adding clothing.

Another specialty is lettering. Drawing letters, for titles, captions, and map labels, is a special craft that requires patience and skill.

PICTURE RESEARCHERS
Picture researchers track down illustrations for magazines. They are familiar with libraries, museums, business firms, and newspapers that have picture collections. The picture researcher must become familiar with the story to be illustrated and must know how and where to find outstanding pictures.

PREPARATION
With a high school diploma it is possible to land a job as a picture researcher or an art department assistant, if you show

Above: the art director doing layout sketches for his magazine. Below: dummy of a magazine page. The magazine is *Sports Illustrated*.

intelligence and talent. With experience you can work up to planning layouts. But progress is faster for those who have been to college or art school. To become an art director, you will probably need art training and considerable experience.

Because you must work closely and smoothly with people inside the office and out, you need a pleasant disposition. As a picture researcher, for example, you must be agreeable if you expect people to let you look through their files of photographs. If you find it difficult to work with others or to take suggestions for improving your work, you may find the magazine field, where working with others is essential, too much of a strain.

You also need what is sometimes called the artist's eye—an ability to choose between a good and an outstanding picture, and to execute pleasing designs.

In addition to formal art training, another way to develop this ability is through photography. Photography as a hobby helps you focus your eyes as well as your lens, and you soon begin to recognize the elements of design.

GETTING STARTED

As a new assistant in the art department you might start out by keeping the picture files in order. In this job you would have a good opportunity to observe all the stages the pictures go through from the time they arrive at the art department until they finally appear in the magazine.

Layout assistants help with **pasting up** (preparation of the dummy). You might occasionally sit in on a presentation, when the art director is showing a layout to the editor for approval.

REWARDS

Art department salaries start at $125 to $165 a week. As you advance to being a layout artist, you can double that, and art directors make $250 to $600 a week or more. Heavily illustrated magazines probably pay more than those using fewer pictures, but they may require more formal training and experience.

Free-lancers who do picture research, retouching, and lettering get paid by the hour, ranging from about five dollars, for simple tasks, up to ten dollars or more for complicated ones.

Advertising Department

The price you pay for your favorite magazine at the newsstand is only a fraction of what it costs to produce. The advertising department supports the magazine and earns the profits by selling advertising space. Production is made possible by advertising dollars. And the job of the people in the advertising department is to bring in those dollars.

ADVERTISING MANAGERS
The advertising manager's job is to plan successful selling campaigns, to stir up enthusiasm among the advertising staff, and to manage the department. Managers help space sellers find new companies to approach and new territories to sell. The manager is an expert in spotting market trends. The department head sometimes receives commissions on increased sales. In any case the sales figures are a measure of the manager's success, so the advertising manager helps the salespeople in every possible way.

SPACE SELLERS
In order to persuade businesses to buy advertising space, salespeople need to be thoroughly familiar with the needs of the business firms. They also need to know their own magazines. Are the readers of the magazine young homemakers, electrical engineers, or sports enthusiasts? Why is this magazine a good place for a particular business to advertise? You

never stop being a student when you sell advertising space. You study what your magazine has to offer and whether or not the advertiser can profit by it. You must be able to quote to prospective advertisers all sorts of figures on your readers: their age level, ethnic background, education, and buying habits.

PREPARATION

Advertising managers and space sellers are usually persuasive people who are able to express themselves with clarity and forcefulness. An ability to write is helpful, too. Some individuals seem to be born salespeople, and if you are one of them, you can probably find a selling job without a college degree. However, you will find work more easily and advance more rapidly if, in addition to sales ability, you have a college education. Selling experience of any sort will also be good preparation for you. The publisher of one large-circulation magazine, says, "It's a selling business, and you need the imagination and scope to understand other peoples' industries and needs."

GETTING STARTED

As a beginner in the advertising department you won't immediately go out and try to convince firms to advertise in your magazine. You may take a hand in market research and analysis. This might include mail or telephone surveys of your readers or of possible advertisers. People good in mathematics are useful in studying the results of such surveys. And in performing this work you will be learning how the advertising department functions.

Magazines too small to have their own advertising departments turn to firms that handle space selling for many magazines. One way to get a start is to work for one of these firms. The experience you get there may help you get a job with a magazine later on.

REWARDS

Because space sales support most magazines, employees in advertising departments are among the best paid in the

magazine field. Beginners may start at less than $200 a week, but experienced space sellers earn $400 a week or more. Managers may receive close to $2,000 a week.

Although advertising people are well paid, they may also find themselves out of jobs more quickly than editorial or art department people. In this field, results are measured in dollars, and advertising managers aren't likely to waste lengthy training periods on salespeople who don't make sales.

Pasting up a magazine dummy.

Production Department

After the editors have prepared copy and the advertising department has sold space, the copy and the ads must go to the printer on schedule. The printed material (proofs) must be proofread, corrected, and returned to the printer on time. Engravers prepare proofs of artwork, and these must be checked and delivered to the right people in time to meet deadlines. On a very small magazine, the editor makes sure that everything is on time. Larger magazines have special departments—production—to handle this work.

PRODUCTION MANAGERS
Production managers on magazines are jugglers. They try to see that everything moves smoothly and that all deadlines are met. They keep charts showing when each step should be taken, and they check with "edit," art people, and the advertising department to make sure that schedules will be followed. They also work with printers and other outside firms. They prod and plead and threaten when necessary to make sure the magazine comes out on time.

Editors and art department heads submit cost estimates. But it is the production chief who brings these figures together

**Editors use colored pencils
so corrections will stand
out clearly for the printer.**

with the prices quoted by outside firms, and keeps a continual check on expenses.

Good production managers read about the field, go to conferences, and seek ways to hold down expenses. They investigate new methods of printing and new paper products.

PRODUCTION ASSISTANTS

In addition to schedules and costs, the production department is responsible for keeping track of all the edit and advertising material as it moves to and from the printer or the engraver. This is a time-consuming job and a crucial one. It is usually handled by assistants in the production department. It requires accuracy and attention to detail.

PREPARATION

If you think you're interested in production, try to get on the staff of your school publication. If your school has a printing shop, by all means take a course. Math and accounting will also help you in your future work.

You can become a production assistant with a high school education, and you may advance once you've proved your ability. But, for the top jobs, publishers often choose people with business school training or college degrees.

GETTING STARTED

There is a great deal of clerical work to be done in the production department. As a beginner in a clerical job, you will be in a position to learn about many of the steps in the publishing process. You will find out about printing costs, and why a cover must close (go to the printer) weeks before the rest of the magazine goes to press. It's all good on-the-job training for a future production manager.

REWARDS

New employees start at about $135 a week. As assistants their earnings rise to $160 or more. A person with lots of experience and a record for getting results can become a production manager earning $700 a week or more.

Circulation and Promotion

The job of these departments is to publicize the magazine in ways that will appeal to new readers and to advertisers.

CIRCULATION

General magazines are usually sold at retail outlets (news-stands, supermarkets, drugstores), and by subscription. The circulation department is concerned with finding new readers for the magazine and at the same time with expanding its readership in certain groups. For example: a manufacturer of tires wants to buy space in a magazine if the readers of the magazine are car-owners, but not if they are people who ride city buses. By the same token, a travel magazine is a likely place for airline and hotel ads. Its circulation manager does not especially want to attract new readers who are stay-at-homes. So while circulation is a "numbers game," it is a highly specialized one. Much of the work involves statistics and **market analysis** (study of the buyers). Lists of names are bought from brokers who are specialists in this field. A magazine stressing the arts might buy a list of the people who have subscribed to a concert series, or are museum-goers.

Circulation letters are mailed out to possible new subscribers, and records are kept of the numbers of people who subscribe as a result. These letters often include cut-rate offers to those who subscribe before a certain date.

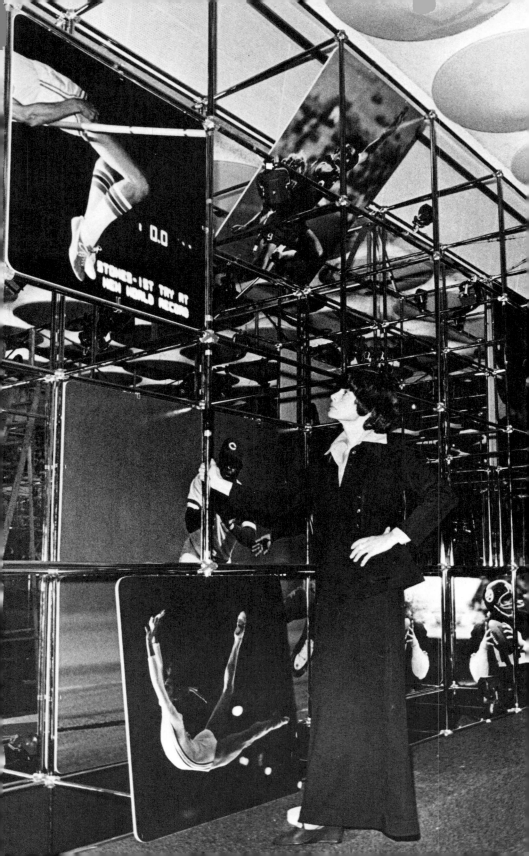

Renewal letters are mailed to readers whose subscriptions are about to expire. Again, careful records are kept of how well each letter worked. As you can see, there are many clerical, statistical, and research jobs in the circulation department. One recent study showed that people were more likely to subscribe if the return card included a stamp to be pasted on a certain spot. Evidently the fun of licking the stamp was enough to persuade them to become subscribers.

The circulation department is also in charge of getting copies of the magazine to newsstands and other retail outlets. This is usually done by contracting with local or regional distribution outfits.

PROMOTION

The goal of the promotion department is to keep the magazine in the news. This is accomplished by sending out news releases, arranging press conferences, having editors appear on talk shows, furnishing speakers to organizations, and setting up displays at conferences. When an employee receives an award, stories are sent to the papers. When a well-known author writes something for the magazine, the promotion people may arrange a luncheon where the author will speak.

Promotion is also directed at possible advertisers in the magazine. Some of the magazine ads you see in newspapers are aimed less at you the reader than at the advertisers who will support the magazine. You will notice that these ads have a lot to say about what kinds of readers the magazine has and about their buying habits. The *"Cosmopolitan* girl," for example, is not only young and beautiful—she also wears makeup and perfume, uses a hairdryer, and buys wines and records.

The press information director checking placement of photographs at a promotional display.

PREPARATION
A good background in mathematics and statistics is useful in circulation. A college degree in business management will be of value to anyone aiming for the top. Writing ability and a lively imagination are essential in promotion work.

GETTING STARTED
Promotion and circulation departments hire trainees and assistants from time to time, with trainees starting on clerical tasks and assistants taking some responsible work off the hands of the department heads. In either position you will be getting on-the-job training, which will enable you to move upward as you learn.

REWARDS
Circulation and promotion beginners earn $125 to $150 a week, while assistants with enough experience to save their bosses time and effort can earn more than $200 a week. The top people in the field receive $400 to $800 a week.

BOOK
PUBLISHING

About Books

When you walk into a bookstore, you find hundreds of books on dozens of different subjects. Books of a certain type or on a particular subject are grouped together. Novels are in one place, cookbooks in another, mysteries in a third.

PUBLISHING HOUSES

The businesses that produce these books are called publishing houses. They all differ from one another. Some publishers bring out hundreds of titles each year. Doubleday, in New York, averages three a day. Other publishers bring out just a handful.

Firms that bring out a variety of books are general publishers. Those that work in a limited area are specialists. Specialized publishers may limit themselves to children's books, law books, medical books, or books in any one of a dozen other categories.

Some publishers produce only hardcover books while others specialize in paperbacks. And some publishing houses produce both. Although the books may be quite different from one another and the publishing houses that produce them may be large or small, the publishing methods are similar and so are the job opportunities.

JOBS

This book will describe the jobs in a large, general publishing house. Smaller firms do the same work, but one person may handle more than one job. A copyeditor may also check proofs, for example. An editor may also write publicity releases.

Book publishing firms, like magazines, have many different departments. There is, of course, the editorial department. Working closely with editorial is the design department. Books, like magazines, have to be produced—so there is a production department. Books must be distributed if they are to be read—so there are sales, advertising, and publicity departments. Finally, there is a special sales department called subsidiary rights. We will discuss jobs in each of these departments in the next chapters.

PUBLISHER

In book publishing, the head of the firm is called the publisher. Years ago the publisher's training was usually in the editorial department. That may still occur today, but publishers now are more likely to be drawn from business, legal, or sales channels. However, unlike the magazine publisher—who stays clear of the editorial side—the book publisher still has an editorial role. The editor-in-chief works for him or her, and the publisher plays an important part in determining what books will be published.

If you are interested in a particular area of publishing—editorial work for example—it would be a good idea to read the section on magazine editorial work as well as the one on editorial departments of book publishers. The work is not identical, but it is similar, and you will have a better picture of job opportunities if you read about both of them.

Editorial Department

Some book publishers have a single editorial department while others have a number of them—children's books, textbooks, mysteries, science fiction—with an editor in charge of each one.

EDITORS

Editors work on many different books at the same time so they have a variety of duties. Let's take a look at an editor at work on a typical day.

The first thing on the editor's schedule may be meeting with a writer to talk about a book the author is about to write. Then, the head of the design department comes by to discuss the pictures for a career guide like this one. When the morning mail arrives, there is a completed **manuscript** (a typewritten copy of a writer's work) to be edited. The editor tackles it immediately and discovers, among other things, that it is much too long. It will be necessary to cut it considerably. At lunchtime the editor has to put the manuscript aside, to keep a lunch date with a literary agent. The agent has discovered a promising young writer. After lunch the editor drops in on the production department to see if schedules can be rearranged to allow for a delay; a writer is ill and cannot return the galleys of his book on time. Then the editor goes into a huddle with the advertising manager to talk about the best possible sales campaign for a book that has just gone

to the printer. Later that afternoon there is a conference in the sales department to discuss a jacket design for a new mystery. And that evening the editor goes home with a bulging briefcase of manuscripts to be read.

EDITORIAL ASSISTANTS

Meanwhile, editorial assistants are also busy. One is writing copy about an author to go on the inside flap of a book jacket. Another is phoning a writer to ask (very tactfully) why a promised manuscript is two weeks overdue. An editorial assistant with a free moment is reading a manuscript. It has been sent in by a writer who hopes that the firm will want to publish it. The assistant will write a brief opinion about the book, and if the manuscript is promising, it will be sent on to an editor for a second reading.

COPYEDITORS

A copyeditor, or style editor, is carefully checking a manuscript for consistency of punctuation, grammar, and spelling. When a word can be spelled in more than one way (theater/theatre), the copyeditor makes sure that the same spelling is used throughout the book. (If you find the same word spelled in two different ways in this book, the copyeditor has not done a thorough job. Theater/theatre doesn't count.) Sometimes the copyediting is done by a free-lancer.

RESEARCHERS AND CHECKERS

Another editorial assistant is checking the facts in a manuscript to make sure that what the writer says is correct. This assistant has learned where to find all sorts of information. Is the population of India really three million? The checker will find out.

Editors read countless manuscripts looking for new material that will suit the particular needs of their firms.

PROOFREADERS

Some typewritten copy is about to be sent to the printer, and an assistant is reading it to make sure that no errors have crept in. When **galley proofs** (long printed sheets) of this copy are returned by the printer, they will be proofread again. The same person may handle both jobs.

FREE-LANCERS

Some editorial work is done by **free-lancers.** These are people who are not full-time employees of one publishing house but are hired to do particular assignments. They may do assignments for many different publishers. Among the jobs usually done by free-lancers are: editing anthologies (collections of poems, essays, or stories); translating books from one language to another; abridging (shortening); copyediting and indexing. The index is the alphabetical guide to the book's contents found on the last few pages. Take a look at this book's index. It was done by a free-lancer.

PREPARATION

In an editorial department you are expected to be a word expert. So the best preparation is to concentrate on English and writing courses, and to do a lot of reading. If you don't love books and reading, you may find publishing is not the field for you. Any experience on school publications is an asset. So is part-time or summer work experience related to books—a job in a bookstore or a library, for example. For an editorial job you will profit from a college degree. If you would like to edit children's books, or other picture books, you should also know something about art, because you will be working closely with the design department. Editors also find them-

The managing editor checks some corrected galleys before routing them to the production manager who will send them to the typesetter.

selves working with production so anything you can learn about the printing process will be helpful, although editors often learn this on the job.

GETTING STARTED

Apprenticeship programs exist and college graduates are often hired specifically to be trained for editorial work. You can inquire about such programs by writing to the editors or personnel offices of publishers who are listed in *Literary Market Place* (see Reading List). Courses in the editorial and bookmaking processes can provide background and training to raise your chances for being hired in a "growth" position.

Your first job in the editorial department could be secretarial. Even if the job consists of typing and filing, it will give you a chance to learn a great deal about the field of publishing. Once you have learned enough to handle an assistant's job you can start moving up. If you have ability, it is not a bad way to start. But it is important, if you start this way, to let your employer know from the beginning that you are interested in training as an editor. Some companies look for secretaries with editorial aspirations while others do not. You should always be very clear about your objectives when you are being interviewed for a job.

REWARDS

Beginning salaries in publishing houses are slightly lower than those in the magazine field. Salaries vary greatly, often depending on the size of the publishing house. You may earn from $100 to $150 a week. Assistant editors earn from $10,000 to $12,000 a year and up. Top editors earn $17,000 to $25,000 and up. Some free-lancers—anthology editors, for example—are paid on a royalty basis. A certain percentage of the price of the book goes to them. But most free-lancers are paid a flat fee, based on the length and difficulty of the assignment.

Design Department (Art Department)

Designing a book is planning how it will look as a finished volume, inside and out. The purpose of design is to make the book attractive, easy to read, and marketable.

ART DIRECTORS
The art director is the head of the design department. The most important part of the job is providing effective jacket designs for books. Jacket design can directly affect the sales of a book. Since the choice is such an important one, the art or design director, the editor, and the sales manager may all have a say in it.

A case in point is the jacket design for the best-selling *Jaws*. It was a dramatic drawing of a shark, which became a sort of trademark for the book. *Jaws* would undoubtedly have sold well even without that jacket. But there is no question that the jacket design helped to boost sales.

In a basic sense, the design director's job is to make money for the firm. By running the design department well, finding the right artwork for the interiors of books, providing jackets that sell, and supervising the creation of appropriate book designs, the director plays a significant role. The position is an important one. Some art directors are vice-presidents of their companies.

GRAPHIC DESIGNERS
The graphic designer takes an edited manuscript and makes a

detailed plan, or design, for the printed book. The page layout, the width of the margins, the design of the title page, even the placement, size, and shape of the *folios* (page numbers) are generally planned by the designer.

The designer suggests the typeface to be used. This is important. The written material must fit within an allotted number of pages and allow enough space for chapter breaks and all the material at the beginning and end of a book—the table of contents, title page, index, and so on. The book must look inviting to read, so the age-group of the readers is another consideration. On top of all that it must be attractive, and the design must be appropriate to the subject.

ASSISTANTS

The art director of a large publishing house usually has an assistant who helps by seeing artists, photographers, and designers who are trying to sell their work. These are the free-lancers who provide some of the artwork (drawings and photographs) and some of the book designs used by the design department. The assistant saves time for the art director by looking at their work and picking out the most promising to send on to the art director.

Other assistants handle clerical work, scheduling, and making character counts (determining the exact number of letters and spaces in a manuscript). An accurate count is needed by the graphic designer before he or she can begin work.

PREPARATION

Design—or art—department heads need the same abilities and talents as the art directors of magazines. They need tal-

**The art director is checking
the size of an illustration
for a children's book.**

ent and experience. They must be able to work closely with other people, including authors, artists, editors, and salespeople, in addition to the employees in their own department. Graphic designers need technical knowledge of typography and production of books. Some art schools offer courses in book design. They are very helpful, but they are no substitute for experience. Part-time or summer work is excellent preparation.

GETTING STARTED
As a new employee in a design department you might do clerical work, or you might be an assistant helping to **paste up** mechanicals. You will be learning the work of the design department. You will learn about illustrations, dummies and **mechanicals,** schedules and budgets. One successful art director says, "For those who do not have degrees, it's even more important to be willing to start on the bottom rung. I started as a secretary to an art director, and have always been grateful that I did. It was my chance to learn everything, from the tedious work of typing and filing, on up to my present position as art director."

REWARDS
A designer with a full-time job in publishing earns at least $275 a week, and may earn more than twice that amount. Free-lancers are paid for individual assignments, and good ones earn $20,000 a year or more, depending on how much of their time they want to devote to it. To quote one free-lancer, "A free-lancer's life is not an easy one." Art directors' salaries may run from $280 to $350 a week. As a beginner in a design department you might earn from $125 to $150 a week.

Preparing art for the book dummy.
A proportional scale is used to
figure exactly by what percent the
illustration must be reduced in size.

[45]

Production Department

After the editorial department has prepared the manuscript and the design department has planned the physical book, it is up to the production department to transform their work into a book—such as the book you hold in your hands.

PRODUCTION MANAGER

Two of the production manager's most important jobs are scheduling and keeping track of costs. A large publisher, producing many books, or "titles," has a schedule for each one and a combined schedule for all of them. It is up to the production manager to see that all the deadlines are met. Costs for each book must be carefully estimated in advance, and checked against the estimates after the work has been completed.

The production manager works closely with the printers, compositors and bookbinders. Prices on paper, printing, and binding are obtained from outside firms. The manager chooses between them on the basis of price, service, and quality.

These are galley proofs. The manuscript has been set into type on long sheets. They are carefully marked for corrections and changes by the author, the editor, and the proofreader before the book is finally set into pages.

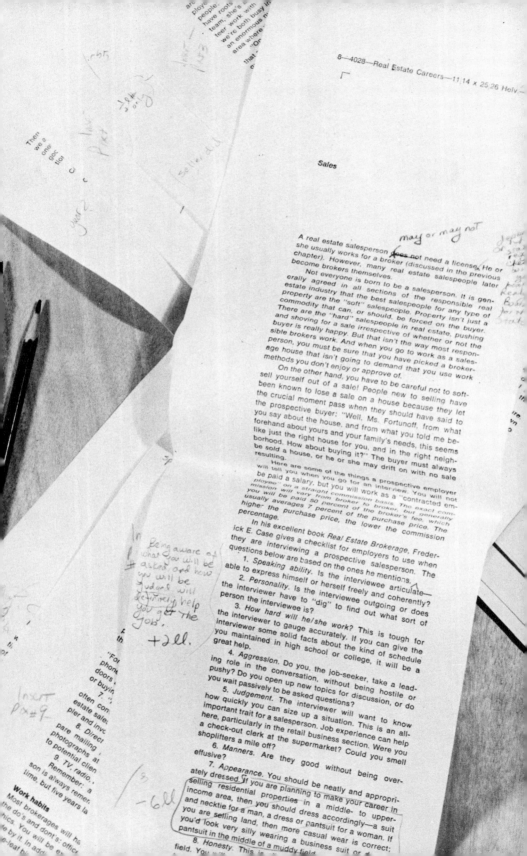

Sales

may or may not

A real estate salesperson ~~does~~ not need a license. He or she usually works for a broker (discussed in the previous chapter). However, many real estate salespeople later become brokers themselves.

Not everyone is born to be a salesperson. It is generally agreed in all sections of the responsible real estate industry that the best salespeople for any type of property are the "soft" salespeople. Property isn't just a commodity that can, or should, be forced on the buyer. There are the "hard" salespeople in real estate, pushing and shoving for a sale irrespective of whether or not the buyer is really happy. But that isn't the way most responsible brokers work. And when you go to work as a salesperson, you must be sure that you have picked a broker-age house that isn't going to demand that you use work methods you don't enjoy or approve of.

On the other hand, you have to be careful not to soft-sell yourself out of a sale! People new to selling have been known to lose a sale on a house because they let the crucial moment pass when they should have said to the prospective buyer: "Well, Ms. Fortunoff, from what you say about the house, and from what you told me be-forehand about yours and your family's needs, this seems like just the right house for you, and in the right neigh-borhood. How about buying it?" The buyer must always be sold a house, or he or she may drift on with no sale resulting.

Here are some of the things a prospective employer will tell you when you go for an interview. You will not be paid a salary, but you will work as a "contracted em-ployee" on a straight commission basis. The exact com-mission will vary from broker to broker, but generally you will be paid 50 percent of the broker's fee, which usually averages 7 percent of the purchase price. The higher the purchase price, the lower the commission percentage.

In his excellent book *Real Estate Brokerage*, Freder-ick E. Case gives a checklist for employers to use when they are interviewing a prospective salesperson. The questions below are based on the ones he mentions.

1. *Speaking ability.* Is the interviewee articulate—able to express himself or herself freely and coherently?

2. *Personality.* Is the interviewee outgoing or does the interviewer have to "dig" to find out what sort of person the interviewee is?

3. *How hard will he/she work?* This is tough for the interviewer to gauge accurately. If you can give the interviewer some solid facts about the kind of schedule you maintained in high school or college, it will be a great help.

4. *Aggression.* Do you, the job-seeker, take a lead-ing role in the conversation, without being hostile or pushy? Do you open up new topics for discussion, or do you wait passively to be asked questions?

5. *Judgement.* The interviewer will want to know how quickly you can size up a situation. This is an all-important trait for a salesperson. Job experience can help here, particularly in the retail business section. Were you a check-out clerk at the supermarket? Could you smell shoplifters a mile off?

6. *Manners.* Are they good without being over-effusive?

7. *Appearance.* You should be neatly and appropri-ately dressed. If you are planning to make your career in selling residential properties in a middle- to upper-income area, then you should dress accordingly—a suit and necktie for a man, a dress or pantsuit for a woman. If you are selling land, then more casual wear is correct; you'd look very silly wearing a business suit or a pantsuit in the middle of a muddy field.

8. *Honesty.* This ...

[handwritten marginalia:]
Being aware of what you will be asked and how you will be judged will definitely help you get the job.

+2ll.

Insert Pix #9

-6ll.

[partial text left margin:]
"For ... phone ... doors ... or buy ...

often con ... estate sale ... pler and inv ...

8. *Direct* ... pare mailing ... photographs ... to potential clien ... 9. *TV, radio,* ... Remember: a ... son is always remer ... time, but five years la ...

Work habits
Most brokerages will ha ... the do's and dont's: office ... hics. You will be ex ... by it. In add ...

Keeping abreast of new production techniques is an important part of the job.

ASSISTANTS
Much of the work of the production department is technical. Production people in large firms often work with complicated office machinery and computers that are capable of doing everything from setting type to estimating costs—although most publishers set their books at outside typesetters. An understanding of printing methods, paper, and bookbinding is essential.

PREPARATION
A good grounding in math is important if you are considering a career in production. Printing experience is valuable, so a part-time job with a printing establishment would be excellent preparation. Office work would be a good way to start learning about office machinery. A production manager deals with figures and budgets, so courses in accounting and business school training are good preparation.

GETTING STARTED
You might very well start out in a clerical job in production. This will give you a chance to start learning about schedules and costs. With experience you may have a chance to move on from clerical work into the more technical areas of production. Part of your job might be getting cost estimates from outside firms and taking back samples of their work for the production manager to study. These are all ways of learning the trade. If you prove to be an apt pupil, you may eventually become a production manager yourself.

REWARDS
Salaries in book production are a little lower than in the magazine field. The number of books being produced has some influence on salaries, with large publishers paying more than smaller ones. As a beginner you might earn $125 or more a week. Production managers earn $380 a week or more.

Distribution

"A book is a book only when it is read; without a reader it is merely so much paper, glue, and cloth." So says Franklin Speir, advertising consultant, in *What Happens in Book Publishing* by Chandler Grannis.

In order to find readers, books must be distributed. This book didn't arrive at your library under its own steam. A great many people worked to make sure that it would wind up in your hands. These people work in sales, advertising, and publicity. Large publishing houses have separate departments to handle the work in each of these areas.

SALES

The sales manager is one of the key executives in a publishing house because the success or failure of the firm rests in large part on the success of the sales force. The head of the department makes plans for selling each book the firm publishes, working closely with the advertising and publicity departments.

The salespeople who visit bookstores are sometimes called travelers, because they spend so much time on the road. Each traveler has a special territory to cover and visits all the booksellers in his or her area regularly. The salespeople, and the sales manager, are in closer contact with the customer than are most other publishing employees.

Some firms publish a list of books that will be sold only

to schools and libraries. These are called "institutional sales" and there are sales representatives ("sales reps") who specialize in selling to this market. Other sales reps are in charge of "trade sales," which means selling books to retail bookstores. Some books are sold both to institutions and to bookstores, with different sales representatives handling each market.

Sales promotion is a special area of the sales department. The people who work on promotion think up ways to help bookstores sell more books. They design window displays, for example, or posters, or special bookcases that the store owner may use. Another service they offer is mailings that the bookseller may send out to his customers.

ADVERTISING

The job of the advertising department is to make sure that you and I and the bookstore owner and the book reviewer and the librarian all know about the new book that is about to be published.

The advertising manager plans a campaign for each book the firm publishes. This is an enormous job, and must be done on a limited budget. The Ford Motor Company may have twelve new car-models to advertise each year, but the large book publisher has hundreds of new books, and each one appeals to a slightly different reading audience. That is why you almost never see commercials on television for one particular book. The cost would be much too great—perhaps even larger than the total sales for a particular title. Instead, advertisements are run in newspapers and magazines, and in trade journals (special publications that go to librarians, booksellers, or schools).

The promotion and advertising manager looks over the mechanical (the final "shooting copy") of a promotion piece.

The advertising manager works closely with the sales, publicity, and editorial departments. Usually an outside ad agency creates and places the ads. The art from the book jacket is often used in advertisements.

PUBLICITY

Publicity is free advertising. The head of this department works with the editorial, sales, advertising, and sales promotion departments in trying to reach the largest possible number of people.

Book reviews are a valuable kind of free advertising. The publicity department mails copies of the book to regular reviewers, and to trade publications, before the book is put on sale. Along with the review copies go various kinds of information, including a short history of the author and the publication date. **Press releases** (written information about the book or the author) are sent to newspapers in the town where the author grew up, and also perhaps to his or her college or to professional publications in the author's field.

Radio and TV interviews are sometimes arranged and they, too, are a valuable source of free publicity. Sometimes the author is willing to visit bookstores and perhaps to autograph copies of his or her newest book.

PREPARATION

As in most other departments it may be possible to land a job in sales, or promotion, or advertising with only a high school diploma. However, if you want to progress rapidly or aim for the top, business school training, or a college degree, will be a great asset.

GETTING STARTED

Your first job may be mailing out review copies, delivering posters to bookstores, or clipping newspaper ads and book reviews. But from your vantage point on the inside you will also learn how to set up a news conference, or how to tailor a sales campaign for a particular audience. With experience you will move up to a job with more responsibility.

REWARDS

New employees earn about $100 a week and assistants make $135 and up. Travelers earn $200 to $400 a week and may also receive commissions on the sales they make. Heads of departments make $400 a week or more.

Rights Department

The first publisher of a book may sell other publishers the right to publish or "reprint" that book. For example, rights for reprinting may be sold to paperback publishers; foreign publishers may buy rights to translate a book into other languages and distribute it abroad; and book clubs may buy rights to print and distribute their own editions of a book. Chapters of books are sold to newspapers and magazines. These transactions are all known as subsidiary rights sales, and major publishers have special rights departments to handle them.

Subsidiary rights are an important source of income to large publishing houses. Sometimes sales of subsidiary rights actually cover the costs of publishing a book—and result in profits for the publisher and the author.

RIGHTS DIRECTOR
The head of the rights department is a gifted salesperson with a knowledge of books, of the publishing market, of legal matters such as contracts and copyright law, and of human nature. This person specializes in the sale of subsidiary rights and goes in search of markets: paperback publishers; newspapers and magazines; film producers; book clubs; foreign publishers. The sale of paperback rights is usually the most profitable, with book club sales coming next. Serialization can also bring in large sums.

PERMISSIONS

Publishers also receive requests from people who want permission to reprint short passages from a book. Sometimes publishers charge a fee for such permissions, but the person in charge of permissions does not actively seek markets. However, a medium-sized publishing house may receive as many as fifteen requests a day.

The person in charge of permissions may be involved in buying as well as selling. If a publishing company decides to publish an anthology, it will be necessary to get permissions from a long list of other publishers. Often, the same person will handle rights and permissions.

COPYRIGHT

A publishing firm must register the copyright on its books to protect the authors against "pirates" who might reprint them without permission. Each title must be registered for copyright. An assistant in the rights department fills out the required forms and sends them to the copyright office in Washington, D.C. After the book has been published, copies of it are sent to the copyright office. Copyright information is printed on one of the front pages of the book. If you look through the first few pages of this book, you will see the copyright notice there.

REQUIREMENTS

A high school diploma may be sufficient for a person who handles permissions, but if you want to work into subsidiary rights, you will have a better chance with more education. An understanding of copyright law will help, even though most publishers have their own legal advisers. Sales experience, too, is helpful.

GETTING STARTED

Newly hired assistants in the rights department handle clerical jobs—receipts, record keeping, filing. They may also handle copyright-registration and routine requests for permissions.

An assistant is in an ideal spot to learn all the intricacies of this department, from international copyright law to writers' contracts.

REWARDS
Subsidiary rights directors earn from $250 to $500 a week, with those in large publishing houses earning more. Since permissions don't bring in large amounts of money, people who handle them are not among the highest paid in publishing. They may earn from $150 to $250 a week.

**The firm may sell
foreign publishers
the right to print
a foreign edition.
Here is a Franklin
Watts book in both
English and Danish.**

Literary Agencies

A literary agent is the person in the middle. He or she finds buyers for the author's writing and finds manuscripts for the publishers—or writers for their ideas. This works to everyone's advantage. The writer is delighted to find a publisher—and the publisher needs new titles to publish.

The best agents have the talents of good editors. They sometimes tell authors how to improve their manuscripts and make them more acceptable. They know good manuscripts when they see them—and they know the right publishing house for a particular manuscript. When an agent persuades a publisher to accept a manuscript, the agent's fee is a percentage of the money received by the writer. A good contract helps both of them. Yet good agents think of more than money. They keep in mind the personalities and needs of their clients. And they are constantly on the lookout for opportunities for them.

People who head their own literary agencies have sometimes been editors first, or have had other publishing jobs.

Not all work is done in offices. Here a literary agent attends a lecture by an author whose work interests him.

They need to know lots of people in publishing in order to be successful.

PREPARATION

To land a job with a literary agency you will need office skills, since most beginning jobs are clerical or secretarial. A college degree isn't required, but a thorough knowledge of literature will be a great asset. You could make a start by learning to type and by concentrating on English and writing courses.

Literary agencies are a small part of the vast publishing field, so it might be wise to aim for a job in publishing rather than for agency work exclusively. With a good background in publishing you might end up running or owning your own agency.

GETTING STARTED

There are large agencies that hire hundreds of employees and small ones run by only two or three people. Most agencies are listed in the *LMP* (*Literary Market Place*), a guide that is available in the reference room of most libraries.

Agencies are busy places with constantly ringing telephones, bulging mailbags, and dozens of appointments to be kept or canceled. New employees may start right out as assistants. Or they may start as secretaries or clerk-typists. In either of these jobs you are in a perfect spot to learn how an agency operates. Everything from writers' contracts to unpublished manuscripts will pass through your hands. With experience you may advance to an assistant's job, with more responsibility.

REWARDS

As a beginner in an agency, you will earn $100 to $135 a week. As an assistant you might make as much as $225 at a large agency. There are some literary agents who earn from $250 to $400 a week, and others who earn from $500 to $1,000. In this field how much you earn depends on how many manuscripts you place with publishers.

A Final Word

Publishing is an old and honorable occupation. It is also one that is subject to the whim of the marketplace, to advances in technology, and to sudden change. It can use young minds and new ideas.

It is an enormously satisfying trade, partly because it deals with the world of words and ideas, partly because its product, the book or the magazine, can be of value to all of us.

For those who are suited to it, by ability and inclination, it is a happy career choice.

Glossary

Artwork: Any illustrative material, including drawings and photographs, paintings, diagrams, etc.

Caption: Brief copy to accompany a photograph, drawing, etc.

Closing: The time when material must go to the printer. ("The December issue is closing next week.")

Copy: Any written material to be printed.

Dummy: A rough layout of text and illustrative material to show position and general appearance of the whole book or magazine.

External: Magazine publication for the dealers and customers of a business or organization.

Industrial (trade journal): A magazine publication for workers in a single industry.

Folio: Page number. Also, leaf of manuscript or book.

Font: A complete assortment of type of one size and scale.

Free-lancer: A person who works independently on assignments (writing, design, etc.) but is not on the regular payroll.

Galley proofs: Long sheets of paper bearing the manuscript text set into type. Their function is to serve as a check that all text has been correctly set, and to give an opportunity for crucial or necessary changes before the book is printed and bound.

House, publishing house: A book publisher.

House organ: A publication for the employees of a firm or organization.

Layout: The placement of text and pictures to show position and general appearance.

Little magazine: A literary magazine, usually a quarterly (published four times a year), devoted to short stories, essays, poetry, etc.

Manuscript: Typed or handwritten copy of an author's work.

Market analysis: Study of buyers and buying habits.

Mechanical (in books): Final layout of proofs from which pages of a book will be photographed.

Pasteup, pasting up: Preparation of layout, dummy, or mechanical.

Press release: Information distributed to the media—usually for advertising purposes.

Professional journal: Magazine of interest to people in a particular profession.

Staff (Staff writer, staff designer, etc.): A full-time employee.

Reading List

Bailey, Herbert S., Jr. *The Art and Science of Book Publishing.* New York: Harper & Row, 1970.

Cooke, David C. *How Books Are Made.* New York: Dodd, Mead, 1963.

Corwen, Leonard. *Your Future in Publishing.* New York: Richards Rosen Press, 1973.

Dembner, S. Arthur, and Massee, William E., eds. *Modern Circulation Methods.* New York: McGraw-Hill, 1968.

Dessauer, John P. *Book Publishing: What It Is, What It Does.* New York: Bowker, 1974.

Ford, James L. C. *Magazines for Millions: The Story of Specialized Publications.* Carbondale, Ill.: Southern Illinois University Press, 1969.

Grannis, Chandler R. *What Happens in Book Publishing.* New York: Columbia University Press, 1967.

Greenfeld, Howard. *Books: From Writer to Reader.* New York: Crown, 1976.

Gross, Gerald. *Editors on Editing.* New York: Grosset & Dunlap, 1962.

————. *Publishers on Publishing.* New York: Grosset & Dunlap, 1961.

Horton, Louise. *Art Careers.* New York: Franklin Watts, 1975.

Petersen, Clarence. *The Bantam Story: Thirty Years of Paperback Publishing.* New York: Bantam Books, 1970.

Peterson, Theodore. *Magazines in the Twentieth Century.* Urbana, Ill: University of Illinois Press, 1964.

Skillin, Marjorie E., et al. *Words into Type.* Englewood Cliffs, N.J.: Prentice-Hall, 1974.

Solomon, Marc, and Wiener, Norman. *Marketing and Advertising Careers.* New York: Franklin Watts, 1976.

Stein, M. L. *Your Career in Journalism.* New York: Julian Messner, 1965.

Tebbel, John. *Opportunities in Publishing Careers.* Louisville, Ky.: Vocational Guidance Manuals, 1975.

Williams, Gurney. *Writing Careers.* New York: Franklin Watts, 1976.

Wolseley, Roland E. *The Changing Magazine.* New York: Hastings House, 1973.

Wolseley, Roland E. *Understanding Magazines.* Ames, Iowa: Iowa University Press, 1969.

Note: Two reference books that are indispensable in the publishing world are *Literary Market Place,* commonly known as *LMP,* and *The Reader's Guide to Periodical Literature.* Both are available in the reference rooms of most libraries.

Index